Growing Up

Leon Read

W
FRANKLIN WATTS
LONDON • SYDNEY

Contents

Look out for Tiger on the pages of this book. Sometimes he is hiding.

From the moment we are
born we are growing up.

This is me when
I was a baby.

Babies

Babies are very young people.

Babies need
a lot of care.

I help to look
after my
baby sister.

Learning new things

As we grow up we learn to do more things.

We are painting a picture.

I can write my name.

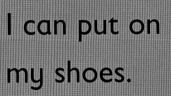

I can put on
my shoes.

I can ride
my bike.

What have you
learned to
do?

Learning from others

We learn things from lots of places.

From books,

from computers,

Teeth

As we grow up we lose our baby teeth.

New teeth push them out.

I gave a tooth
to the tooth fairy
and made a
picture of her.

Why should you
keep your teeth
clean?

Growing tall

As we grow up we get taller.

Helping others

As we grow up we can help others.

I'm helping my little sister build a tower.

I helped to make some flat bread.

When did you last help someone?

15

Thinking and sharing

Tiger will not share his pens
with Rabbit.

He wants to keep them all.

Why should Tiger share?

Now Rabbit can
draw a picture.

Getting older

When we are older we can have babies of our own...

...and even have grandchildren.

I want to be...

It is fun to think about what we will be when we grow up.

I want to be a police officer.

I want to
be a vet.

21

All grown up

Aisha has drawn a
picture of her family.
Now you do the same.

Then draw a picture of you as a grown up.

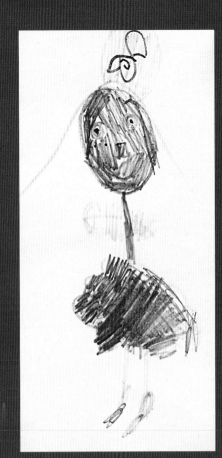

I'm drawing a picture of me as a ballerina.

Word picture bank

Baby – P. 4, 5, 18, 19   Helping – P. 14, 15   Learning – P. 8

Reading – P. 9   Sharing – P. 17   Vet – P. 21

First published in 2007 by Franklin Watts
338 Euston Road, London NW1 3BH

Franklin Watts Australia
Level 17/207 Kent Street, Sydney NSW 2000

Copyright © Franklin Watts 2007

Series editor: Adrian Cole
Photographer: Andy Crawford (unless otherwise credited)
Design: Sphere Design Associates
Art director: Jonathan Hair
Consultants: Prue Goodwin and Karina Law

A CIP catalogue record for this book is available
from the British Library.

ISBN: 978 0 7496 7613 1

Dewey Classification: 612.6

Acknowledgements:
The Publisher would like to thank Norrie Carr model agency
and Scope. 'Tiger' and 'Rabbit' puppets used with kind
permission from Ravensden PLC (www.ravensden.co.uk).
Tiger Talk logo drawn by Kevin Hopgood.

Liz Banfield/Jupiter Images (5t). Knauer/Johnston/Jupiter Images
(5b). Adam Woolfit/Corbis (13t). Bluestone/Science Photo
Library (19).

Every attempt has been made to clear copyright.
Should there be any inadvertent omission please
apply to the publisher for rectification.

Printed in China

Franklin Watts is a division
of Hachette Children's Books,
an Hachette Livre UK company.

There are 20 Tigers, including me, in this book.
Did you find all of us?